Contents

Introduction 2

Chapter 1 Expected Loss and Loan Loss Provisions 4

   1.1 Introduction 4

   1.2 Probability of Default 5

   1.3 Exposure at Default 6

   1.4 Credit Conversion Factor (CCF) 8

   1.5 Loss Given Default 9

   1.6 Expected Loss 11

   1.7 Loan Loss Provision 12

   1.8 Collective and Individual Provisioning 13

   1.9 Loan Loss Provision under IFRS 9 15

Chapter 2 Risk Weighted Assets 17

   2.1 Introduction 17

   2.2 Credit Risk Weighted Assets 20

   2.3 Standardized and Internal Ratings Based Approaches 23

   2.4 Interest Rate Risk RWA – IRRBB RWA 25

   2.5 Markets Risk RWA 26

   2.6 Operational Risk Weighted Assets 29

Summary 30

Source 31

Introduction

Risk weighted assets is the foundation for assessing the risk of unexpected losses of deposit taking financial institutions. As that sentence may have been hard to understand read it again after finishing the book.

This book provides a simple explanation for Risk Weighted Assets for novice bankers as well as bankers who are moving into the Risk domain of a financial institution. It is also relevant for any business having exposure to risk, especially credit risk.

Risk-weighted assets are arrived at from different risk perspectives. These are credit risk, interest rate risk, market risk and operational risk. The methodology used is primarily credit risk driven. The methodology is then extended to arrive at a similar dollar value for interest rate, market and operational risk.

Credit risk can lead to expected loss and unexpected loss. Expected loss is covered by loan-loss provisions and unexpected loss by equity arrived at by risk-weighting assets. Considering risk-weighted assets look at residual risk it is important to understand loan loss provisioning before we get into risk-weighted assets. In case you already understand loan-loss provisioning you can go straight to the chapter on credit risk weighted assets.

To understand **expected risk** and provisioning for **expected losses** we will go into the inputs required for

Loan Loss Provision, namely **Customer Credit Rating**, **Exposure Amount** and **Collateral Quality**. We will also briefly discuss the changes introduced in IFRS 9.

Once an understanding of expected loss is gained we will look at the risk of unexpected losses inherent in Credit assets and the assessment using the Risk Weighted Assets method as prescribed by Basel III.

Following this we will expand Credit RWA to Interest Rate, Market and Operational Risk.

The key topics covered are as follows:

1. Expected Loss and Loan Loss Provisions
2. Credit Risk & CRWA
3. Standardized and Advanced Approaches
4. Interest Rate Risk & IRRWA
5. Market Risk & MRWA
6. Operational Risk & ORWA
7. Summary

Chapter 1 Expected Loss and Loan Loss Provisions

1.1 INTRODUCTION

Credit Risk is the risk of not receiving an amount due to us because of a counterparty's lack of willingness or ability to pay the same. For example, if a loan is given to a corporate, how do you quantify the risk of not getting the principal and interest due to the bank. We say we have an **exposure** to Credit Risk. Just as exposure to the sun leads us to a risk of cancer, lending leaves us exposed to credit risk – the risk of not getting our money back.

As a bank's main business is lending, credit risk primarily includes risk of non-payment of principal and interest.

Credit Risk is quantified by calculating the average of losses seen historically on a loan with similar characteristics. This average is the **Expected Loss** and is calculated on an exposure over a specific period of time. In this chapter we will consider the Expected Loss over a 1-year horizon unless stated otherwise.

1.2 PROBABILITY OF DEFAULT

There are 3 drivers to Expected Loss. The first one is the willingness and ability of the borrower to pay the dues or the **credit quality** of the borrower. The credit quality of the borrower is assessed from the financials of the borrower and loan repayment history. This will tell you about the ability and willingness of a borrower to make his interest and principal repayments. The credit quality of the borrower gives you a view into the probability of a borrower defaulting on his loan. This is referred to as the **Probability of Default (PD)**. Each borrower is assigned a **Credit Rating** in accordance with the PD band that he falls into. The goal of Credit Assessment of a customer is to assign a Credit Rating to the customer aligned to Probability of Default.

Credit assessments are a topic in itself and will not be dealt with here.

Below is shown a sample from S&P ratings and observed average default rates as of 28th Dec 2017[1]:

S&P Rating	AAA	AA+	AA	AA-	A+	A
Observed PD	0.00%	0.00%	0.02%	0.04%	0.06%	0.08%

S&P Rating	A-	BBB+	BBB	BBB-	BB+	BB
Observed PD	0.07%	0.12%	0.19%	0.31%	0.35%	0.53%

S&P Rating	BB-	B+	B	B-	CCC/C
Observed PD	1.06%	2.00%	4.76%	8.47%	27.19%

1.3 EXPOSURE AT DEFAULT

The second driver for Expected Loss is the **Exposure at Default**. This is the amount due to us at the time of default. One option for EAD could be to take the current loan outstanding amount. But we know the amount due to us can change between now and when the default happens. Let us take a simplified example to aid our understanding. A borrower has taken a loan of Rs 40 lacs. He is paying a monthly instalment of Rs 40,000 which includes interest at 10% p.a. Below is a table that shows the loan outstanding amount across the year.

Loan Drawdown			Amount	₹ 40,00,000
Date	01-Jan-18		Interest	10%

Date	EMI	Interest	Principal	Balance
01-Feb-18	₹ 40,000	₹ 33,333	₹ 6,667	₹ 39,93,333
01-Mar-18	₹ 40,000	₹ 33,277	₹ 6,723	₹ 39,86,610
01-Apr-18	₹ 40,000	₹ 33,221	₹ 6,779	₹ 39,79,831
01-May-18	₹ 40,000	₹ 33,165	₹ 6,835	₹ 39,72,996
01-Jun-18	₹ 40,000	₹ 33,108	₹ 6,892	₹ 39,66,104
01-Jul-18	₹ 40,000	₹ 33,050	₹ 6,950	₹ 39,59,154
01-Aug-18	₹ 40,000	₹ 32,992	₹ 7,008	₹ 39,52,146
01-Sep-18	₹ 40,000	₹ 32,934	₹ 7,066	₹ 39,45,080
01-Oct-18	₹ 40,000	₹ 32,875	₹ 7,125	₹ 39,37,955
01-Nov-18	₹ 40,000	₹ 32,816	₹ 7,184	₹ 39,30,771
01-Dec-18	₹ 40,000	₹ 32,756	₹ 7,244	₹ 39,23,527

So yes, even if the loan amount today is 40 lacs, over the course of the next 1 year the outstanding loan amount will go down as the monthly payments are made. So, can we take the average of the daily outstanding loan amount?

Let's consider the date 1st Feb 2018 before the EMI is paid. The borrower owes us the full 40 lacs as well the interest due for the first month which is Rs. 33,333. So, if he defaults on 1st Feb 2018 the **Exposure at Default** would be 40,33,333. Therefore, the daily exposure amount should include the interest accrued or due upto that date. We would also need to consider any fees that could come due. The EAD could thus be calculated as the average of the daily exposures.

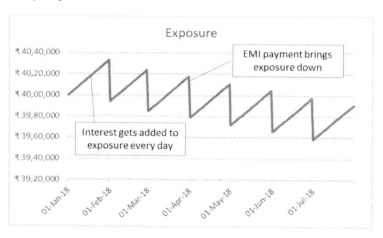

1.4 CREDIT CONVERSION FACTOR (CCF)

Exposure at Default (EAD) is estimated basis the specific characteristics of each asset class. What happens in the case of a Trade Limit of 10 lacs set up for a manufacturing company? Let's say currently the customer has drawn down an amount of 2 lacs. In that case should EAD be 2 lacs, the current exposure? But tomorrow the customer may drawdown up to 10 lacs or bring the balance down to zero. As seen in the last example EAD depends on the average of expected daily exposures over a period of 1 year. It seems logical to say that the current exposure of 2lacs has to be taken as well as a percentage of the undrawn amount. And that's exactly how EAD is calculated - the current drawn down amount plus a percentage of the undrawn limit.

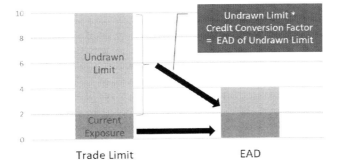

The percentage is arrived at by analysing data for similar asset given to customers in that industry. The percentage applied to the undrawn limit is called the **Credit Conversion Factor** and lets you arrive at the required EAD.

There are other off-balance sheet instruments, as well, like guarantees where credit conversion factor is used.

1.5 LOSS GIVEN DEFAULT

In the last section we came to an understanding of Exposure at Default. So, if the customer defaults, is our Expected Loss equal to the Exposure at Default? Well, it depends on what mitigants you have put in place for such a scenario. First let's take the case of a Home Loan of 40 lacs. You would have taken the house as **collateral**. Hence you can sell the house in case of a default and recover some of the amounts due to you. You may expect to be able to recover 100% of the value considering your loan amount of 40 lacs is only 80% of the value of the house which was 50 lacs at the time of giving out the loan.

Suppose the customers cash flow has taken a hit because of demonetization as the customer's customers are scrambling to make digital payments. The customer is unable to make the EMI payments for three months and the bank values the property for the potential sale against default. However, of course, property values have also fluctuated and the expected value of the property has dropped considerably. So, in case the default happens after 6 months and EAD is Rs 40,10,000 as the customer did not pay last three months interest due. On the other hand, suppose the property value has dropped 30%. So, although you had given the loan at 80% loan to value ratio, you are selling a house which was originally 50 lacs at 35 lacs thus incurring a loss.

Hence,

Loss = Exposure at Default – Collateral Value

= 40,10,000 – 35,00,000 = 5, 10,000

In this particular case

LGD = 5,10,000/40,10,000 = = 12.7%

We have taken one specific example above to get a sense of how LGD is calculated.

Loss Given Default is calculated as the ratio of Loss to Exposure at Default using historical loss data for a particular asset class with a specific type of collateral. Then the LGD ratio is used to calculate the expected loss on the loan portfolio.

1.6 EXPECTED LOSS

Now that we understand EAD, PD and LGD we are ready to calculate Expected Loss (EL).

Expected Loss is calculated as Exposure at Default multiplied by Loss Given Default ratio into the Probability of Default.

$EL = PD * EAD * LGD$

Probability of Default, PD's driver is Credit Quality of the customer which is converted to a Credit Rating during Credit Assessment. Hence PD is driven by the *customer* credit quality.

Exposure at Default, EAD, is a characteristic of the *asset product* which gives rise to the exposure: Home Loan, Trade Limit, Guarantee, Working Capital Loan, Long Term Corporate Loan, Over draft etc.

Loss Given Default, LGD, depends on the security or *collateral* arrangements you have made that mitigate the credit risk.

1.7 LOAN LOSS PROVISION

Loan Loss Provision, LLP, is the amount kept aside by a bank from its revenue to cover the Expected Loss over a period of time – typically for the next one year. Hence it is an annual expense for the bank. Let's say at the end of the previous year the Expected Loss on the portfolio for the next year was calculated as 1 Crore. The actual loss this year was 60 lacs. Hence, there is a balance of 40 lacs in provisions. If the portfolio now has been calculated to have an expected loss for the next year of 90 lacs. Then we will need to put in 50 lacs as provision expense to bring the provision up to the level required of 90 lacs.

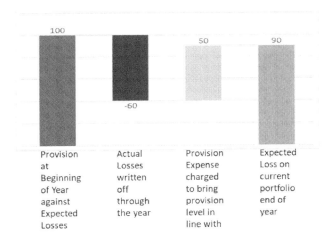

| Provision at Beginning of Year against Expected Losses | Actual Losses written off through the year | Provision Expense charged to bring provision level in line with | Expected Loss on current portfolio end of year |

Loan Loss Provision is the amount you have set aside for Expected Losses; and Provision Expense or Charge is the amount that you need to set aside additionally due to actual losses and changes in Provision required due to change in underlying portfolio.

1.8 COLLECTIVE AND INDIVIDUAL PROVISIONING

A bank can have a portfolio of thousands of loans. Instead of calculating the provisions for each loan separately a portfolio approach is taken. Each asset class is assigned a basis for calculating the EAD and each collateral type is assigned an LGD from historical data. Then the provision can be calculated as

$$EAD * LGD * PD$$

where PD would be dependent on the customer credit rating. The provision calculated in this manner for the portfolio as a whole is called **Collective Provisioning** and is applicable for cases where the probability of default is low. This means that as long as the customer credit rating is good, collective provisioning is sufficient.

The customer credit rating is reviewed periodically. It is also reviewed in case of any credit event like non-payment of interest or principal payments, non-payment of dues to other banks, vendors or employees. In such case credit rating of the customer will be downgraded and if it is found that the customer credit quality has deteriorated to such an extent that the probability of default has become higher than 25% it is time to assess the exposure individually. The specific characteristics of the exposure is assessed to arrive at an Exposure at Default and the specific characteristics of the collateral is assessed to arrive at LGD.

For example, say a home loan has been given. As long as customer is regular in payments of EMIs provisioning for the loan is done at a collective level. But in case the customer has missed payments for three months consecutively it is time for a credit review of the customer. On review if we find that the customer is facing financial distress we downgrade the customer credit rating and go in for Individual Provisioning. This leads to an assessment of the property value and calculation of the loss amount in case of default of the specific loan as well as any other exposure to the customer.

The collateral value will be monitored on a more frequent basis. The calculation of provision at a customer level is called **Individual Provisioning**.

1.9 LOAN LOSS PROVISION UNDER IFRS 9

Prior to IFRS 9, Loan Loss Provisioning was over a 1-year horizon. This means the provisioning was for expected losses in the next 12 months.

With IFRS 9 loan loss provisioning continues to be over a 1-year horizon unless the credit rating has deteriorated. In case the credit rating has deteriorated but not enough to warrant Individual Provisioning then in certain cases Loan Loss Provision will need to be taken for expected losses over the life of the asset.

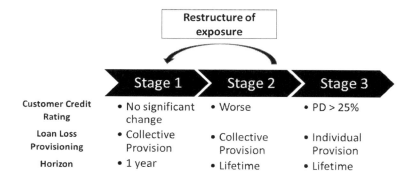

Stage 1: When a loan has been newly given out it falls under Stage 1. The loan has been structured with collateral and pricing in line with the risk underlying the exposure. Collective provision is taken for expected losses in the next 12 months.

Stage 2: If the credit rating significantly worsens from the time of initial loan or limit approval, the provisioning has to cover losses expected over the life of the exposure – loan tenor. The asset can be reclassified to Stage 1 if the loan is restructured by bringing the collateral and pricing in line with the higher risk.

Stage 3: This is same as the individual provisioning which was applicable earlier also. Individual provisioning remains over the lifetime of the loan.

Chapter 2 Risk Weighted Assets

2.1 INTRODUCTION

Loan Loss Provisioning covers expected losses from a bank's exposure. But this covers losses only in some of the years as shown in the graph below for a sample data set. Since, expected loss is an average there will of course be times when loss is more than the provision set aside for expected loss.

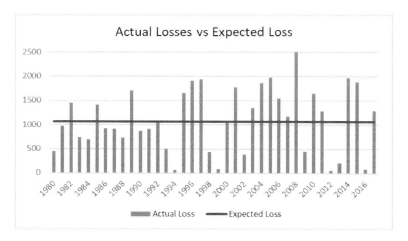

What happens in the years where Actual Loss is more than the expected loss? We have an **Unexpected Loss**. Expected Losses are covered by provisions. What about unexpected losses?

We cannot say that unexpected losses will even out in the long run, because in the short run it will impact our liquidity and our ability to release funds to deposit holders as and when they ask for the same. Hence, the regulators have said that a bank needs to keep sufficient equity to cover unexpected losses. This means that in a downturn, investors will lose money before a depositor will, ensuring excessive risk is not taken by a bank focussed only on maximizing returns.

In the graph below the top half of the graph is the unexpected losses to be covered by equity.

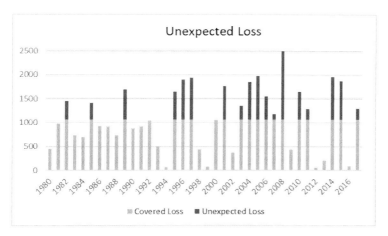

How do we calculate the equity to be kept aside for such downturn scenarios? As per Basel I the requirement was to keep aside a fixed 8% of the overall exposure of the bank. However, this did not consider the risk profile of the assets. Let's say on the one hand we have a 20-lac personal loan given to an individual with no security or collateral. On the other hand, we have a 20-lac home loan given at a loan to value ratio of 50%, i.e. the loan amount is 50% of the valuation of the house mortgaged to the bank. Is the unexpected loss covered by keeping aside 8% of the loan value – 1.6lacs - in both cases? Or should we be keeping more for the personal loan and less for the home loan considering the difference in risk between the two assets?

Risk Weighting Assets allows you to arrive at an asset value in line with the underlying risk of the asset and not just the value of the exposure, allowing for a more sensitive calculation of the equity required for covering unexpected losses. Unexpected losses from the name itself will give you the idea that it can go up to 100 % of the exposure in worst case scenarios. Although having that level of equity will make deposits 100% protected from credit risk, it will mean that returns to shareholders will be very low. Hence a cut-off is taken for covering 99.9% of unexpected losses with the government expected to support in the worst-case scenario.

The concept of Risk Weighted Assets can be extended to Operational and Market Risk over and above the obvious application in Credit Risk. We will look at all three in the next few sections.

2.2 CREDIT RISK WEIGHTED ASSETS

Credit Risk Weighted Assets (CRWA) is a calculated value that allows you to arrive at the equity required for covering unexpected losses. An exposure of Rs 10 lac can give rise to a CRWA value of Rs 20 lac, Rs 10 lac or Rs 1 lac depending on the credit risk of the asset allowing you to arrive at equity required in line with the risk of the asset rather than the exposure value.

Let's take a few concrete examples to get a sense of how portfolio level CRWA calculations are done.

First example is of a home loan - the most common medium risk asset. You have given a home loan of 40 lacs against a property worth 50 lacs as collateral. This means that the loan to value ratio is 80%. The maximum exposure in the next one year is 44lacs given a 10% interest payable per annum. So maximum EAD is 44 lacs.

If you skipped the provisions section and are finding this hard to follow you may want to revisit the first chapter.

What about LGD (Loss Given Default)? Property values can fall depending on the market. And worst-case scenario, a beach front property can be wiped out in a tsunami. So minimum property value can actually be zero. But what is the probability that such an event would happen? Let's say it is less than 0.1%. Which means that in the last 1000 years a catastrophic event has not happened that wiped out the value of the property completely. Or in the last 5 years history of giving loans less than 1 in 1000 properties values have fallen to zero. So, we can say with a confidence of 99.9% that value of property will not fall to zero. Let's say, when we look at the portfolio for the last 5 years less than 1 in 1000 properties have had their price fall by more than 50%. This means that we can say with 99.9% confidence the property price will not fall below 25 lacs. Then our loss given default will not be more than 19lacs (44 lacs – 25 lacs) as we will be able to recover 25 lacs by selling the house.

What about probability of default?

Let's say that we are 99.95 % sure that not more than 85 will default out of every 1000 loans given out? Then our probability of unexpected loss is 8.5%. In which case for every loan of 40 lacs we need to keep aside equity of 1.6lacs (8.5% of 19lacs).

Similarly let's say we have a Corporate Loan of 40 lacs and we arrive at an equity requirement of 3.2 lacs.

Next, we have a credit card exposure of 40 lacs for which the equity required has been calculated as 8 lacs.

Finally, we have a personal loan of 40 lacs taken against a Time Deposit of 60 lacs. Hence required equity is zero lacs.

Now if we say that we have a credit exposure of 40lacs we are not really conveying the underlying credit risk we are carrying. Depending on the asset class the risk will differ because of which the equity to be held varies from 0 lacs to 8 lacs in our examples above depending on the asset class.

Prior to Basel II and the introduction of RWA, equity set aside for unexpected losses was 8% of the bank's exposure. In the examples seen above the corporate loan fits that category and the equity required is 8% of exposure. So, the corporate loan's exposure amount is considered to be equal to its risk weighted asset value. The exposure amount correctly reflects its unexpected risk.

If you consider the home loan the unexpected loss is half that of the corporate loan. Accordingly, it is equivalent to a 20 lacs corporate loan. Hence risk weighted asset value of a home loan is 20 lacs. A credit card is way riskier than both corporate loan and home loan and TD secured loan is not risky at all and has an RWA of 0 lacs.

Table: Loans of **40 lacs** with different RWA

Type	**Unexpected Loss (99.9%)**	**Equity %**	**RWA**	**RWA %**
Corporate Loan	3.2 lacs	8%	40 lacs	100%
Home Loan	1.6 lacs	4%	20 lacs	50%
Credit Card	8 lacs	20%	100 lacs	250%
TD Secured	0 lacs	0%	0 lacs	0%

So, when we compare the books of two banks the relative credit risk can be compared accurately using the CRWA value rather than the total asset value.

Thus, we have been able to arrive at a much more sensitive and elegant way of capturing the underlying risk of each asset class.

2.3 STANDARDIZED AND INTERNAL RATINGS BASED APPROACHES

To calculate RWA, Basel norms provide standard risk weights for different asset classes. All banks have the option of using these norms. Some sample weights are given below:

Asset Class	Risk Weight
Loans Secured by residential property	35%
Other retail loans	75%
Loans to corporate with AAA rating	20%
Loans to corporates with rating below B-	150%

As you can see this simplifies calculations and we do not need to get into the analysis of historical portfolios to arrive at RWA. You just provide the Risk Weights provided by Basel norms which have been arrived at by doing comprehensive analysis.

However, as a bank you may have in place mitigants to the credit risk, reducing the equity requirement considerably. In such case you can opt for the internal ratings based (IRB) approach for which you would need to get the approval of local regulators.

In Foundation IRB you assess your customers and arrive at your own Credit Rating and Probability of Default but use the EAD, LGD and other parameters as prescribed by Basel.

Under Advanced-IRB you can build the model completely defining all the parameters from your side.

Each bank divides its asset portfolio in line with the approach used to arrive at RWA - standardized approach, Foundation IRB and Advanced IRB approach.

Country regulators may also propose their own slotting approach to determine capital requirements within the IRB approach.

2.4 INTEREST RATE RISK RWA – IRRBB RWA

The key risk that a bank takes is credit risk. This is the core business of the bank. The second key risk is interest rate risk.

The loan portfolio tends to have tenors of up to 10 years whereas the deposit portfolio is highly weighted towards tenors of less than 1 year. Hence the bank runs the risk of interest rates going up leading to higher cost of funds. This risk is called Interest Rate Risk in the Banking Book (IRRBB). There is also interest rate risk in the trading book that will be covered under Markets Risk RWA.

Expected impact of interest rate risk is covered by pricing of the assets. However, for any unexpected losses, like we had for credit risk, we need to set aside equity.

If you relook at the table on page 17 you will see that,

RWA * 8% = Equity required to cover unexpected loss

Rearranging the equation, we get

RWA = Unexpected loss * 1/8% = Unexpected Loss * 12.5

Hence if we are able to arrive at unexpected losses from interest rate risk in the banking book, we can also arrive at the Interest Rate Risk RWA.

2.5 MARKETS RISK RWA

Market risk refers to loss due to change in valuation of trading book assets. There are three main risks here. First is that the valuation of the asset is lower than expected due to which bank is liable to pay the difference to the customer. Typically expected volatility is priced into the product. However unexpected volatility can lead to higher than expected losses in a particular period. This is the standard definition of Market Risk and we need to set aside equity for this which we can back calculate as follows. The unexpected loss calculation will of course take a book of its own to cover.

RWA = Unexpected loss * 1/8% = Unexpected Loss * 12.5

Hence if we are able to arrive at unexpected Market Losses we can also arrive at the Market RWA.

There is also a Credit Risk associated to market products. In case the bank is in the money, the customer owes the bank and there arises a possibility of default on the side of the customer. The Credit Risk RWA associated with market products is calculated in a similar way to loans. So PD, LGD and EAD come into the picture. The formula also includes the impact of volatility on the losses.

The third risk associated with Market products is Interest Rate Risk. You have given an interest rate swap to a customer allowing him to convert floating rate to fixed rate of interest. Now this is a risk the bank has taken separate from any lending and is called the interest rate risk of the trading book. And an associated RWA is calculated against this risk.

In the 2007-2008 Global Financial Crisis primary losses were driven by market risk. But this led to impact on the books of other banks as well as corporates leading to Credit Default.

Market risk is not associated with any assets or lending. Hence, they do not appear on the balance sheet. These are called off balance sheet items.

With Basel III it has become necessary to calculate Market Risk RWA and make it a part of Pillar III disclosure.

2.6 OPERATIONAL RISK WEIGHTED ASSETS

Basel III requires that we quantify not only the Credit risk of a bank but also market and operational risk. Operational risk has become particularly significant due to the dependence we have on technology and the probability of fraud, data breaches and the fact that technological glitches can wipe out huge amounts.

Accordingly, banks are expected to quantify unexpected operational losses and set aside equity for the same. The equity requirement is converted to an Operational RWA number so we can arrive at the overall risk that a bank is facing.

An excerpt from the submission by ANZ in June 2018 is shown below:

Risk Weighted Assets (RWA)	Jun 18 $M
Subject to Advanced Internal Rating Based (IRB) approach	
Corporate	122,902
Sovereign	7,112
Bank	15,083
Residential Mortgage	99,257
Qualifying Revolving Retail	6,679
Other Retail	29,992
Credit risk weighted assets subject to Advanced IRB approach	**281,025**
Credit Risk Specialised Lending exposures subject to slotting approach[1]	32,714
Subject to Standardised approach	
Corporate	14,085
Residential Mortgage	326
Other Retail	95
Credit risk weighted assets subject to Standardised approach	**14,506**
Credit Valuation Adjustment and Qualifying Central Counterparties	7,633
Credit risk weighted assets relating to securitisation exposures	1,716
Other assets	3,310
Total credit risk weighted assets	**340,904**
Market risk weighted assets	7,181
Operational risk weighted assets	37,378
Interest rate risk in the banking book (IRRBB) risk weighted assets	8,988
Total Risk Weighted Assets	**394,451**

Summary

- Loan loss provision is taken by the bank to cover for expected credit losses
- Loan loss provision is calculated as Probability of Default * Exposure at Default * Loss Given Default (%)
- Probability of Default (PD) reflects the Credit Rating of the borrower / counterparty which quantifies their ability and willingness to pay dues
- Exposure at Default (EAD) is calculated as the average of daily expected exposure over the period
- Loss Given Default (LGD) takes into account the collateral or security available to cover for losses
- Shareholder Equity is required to cover unexpected losses 99.9% of the time
- Risk Weighted Asset value quantifies the risk of unexpected loss
- RWA is calculated for unexpected losses from Credit Risk, Interest rate risk, Market Risk and Operational Risk in line with Basel III

Source

1. Basel III: A Global Regulatory Framework for more resilient banks and banking systems

   htttps://www.bis.org/publ/bcbs189.pdf

2. Credit Research Initiative, National University of Singapore

   http://d.rmicri.org/static/pdf/Probability%20of%20Default%20Implied%20Rating%20White%20Paper.pdf

3. ANZ June 2018 Pillar III Disclosure

   http://shareholder.anz.com/sites/default/files/anzs_june_2018_pillar_3_disclosure.pdf